P9-CEX-304

Geiger

01

DATE			
MAR 28	OCT 9		
MAY 7	FEB 4		
OCT 22	Copp		
MAY 12	NOV		
Noyer	OCT 22		
SEP 23	NOV. 11		
DEC 9			
SEP 16			
OCT 20			
SEP 18			
OCT 8			

THE
CROW INDIANS

THE
CROW INDIANS

HUNTERS OF THE
NORTHERN PLAINS

By SONIA BLEEKER

Illustrated by Althea Karr

WILLIAM MORROW & COMPANY
New York · 1953

Twelfth Printing

Grateful recognition is given to
Professor Robert H. Lowie,
Department of Anthropology, University of California,
for reading and criticizing the manuscript.

CONTENTS

CONTENTS

THE
CROW INDIANS

1

THE WAR PARTY

THE large Crow camp by the Little Horn River in southeastern Montana was as full of activity as a beehive. Horsemen dashed up to the tipis, dismounted, and disappeared into them. Children raced about. Dogs barked.

The hundred skin-covered tipis that made up

the camp spread wide over the rolling prairie. Above, on the ends of the long, thin tipi poles, streamers of fringed buckskin waved gaily in the breeze. Ribbons of smoke curled upward from almost every tipi and faded into the clear, warm sky. Narrow flaps of buffalo skin, stretched on two poles, covered the openings of each tipi. These flaps slapped back and forth as horsemen dismounted and entered the tipis. They slapped open again as the men came out, sprang on their horses, and galloped away.

This was the first warm day of spring. The Crow called it the first day of summer, since they divided the year into two main seasons: summer and winter. The Crow lands in the northern plains were hot in summer and very cold in winter. Other Indian tribes lived near the Crow. All, including the Crow, were Indians of the Plains. They all hunted the buffalo, on which they depended. With some tribes, such as the Hidatsa and Mandan to the east, the Crow lived and traded in peace. In fact, a few centuries before, the Hidatsa and the Crow were one people. For reasons we still do not know they split up, and the

Crow moved westward. Much later they separated into two large groups: River Crow and Mountain Crow. The name *Crow* comes from the Indian word *Absaroka*, which means crow, sparrow hawk, or bird people.

But the Crow warred with the Blackfoot to the north, with the Dakota to the east, and with the Cheyenne to the south. These tribes had been their enemies since ancient times. It may be that the Cheyenne and Dakota tried to keep the Crow from entering their buffalo lands when the Crow first moved westward. The powerful Cheyenne and Dakota far outnumbered the small Crow tribe, which at that time numbered about three thousand people. However, they were fearless warriors and kept their enemies constantly on guard.

Now that the ground was free of snow, the men could ride their sturdy ponies about the camp, instead of bucking the knee-deep drifts on foot or on snowshoes. The men looked their best on horseback. They were tall, lean hunters, many of them six feet tall or more. All wore buckskin shirts and fringed leggings and moccasins. The shirts, leggings, and moccasins were heavily embroidered with porcupine quills, in bright stripes of red, yellow, and purple. Each hunter carried a bow and a quiverful of arrows. A war club or bone knife was tucked into the wide, embroidered buckskin belt. The men's hair, glossy with bear grease, was parted neatly in the center over their narrow foreheads. A long braid hung on each shoulder, reaching well below the waist. The men took great pride in their long hair, which was often even longer than the women's.

The Crow had full brown faces with high cheekbones. Their dark eyes were narrow and their noses long and straight. Everyone wore ornaments: earrings of bone and shell; necklaces of shell, of beaver, bear, and elk teeth, or bear claws. Most men had one or two grayish-black, white-tipped eagle feathers stuck in a knot of hair on the back of the head.

These horsemen of the northern plains were seldom seen traveling on foot in summer. Even when they had to go from one end of their camp to the other, they mounted their swift horses.

On this warm spring day the riders were all

men. The women and girls were busy inside the tipis by the small fires, preparing meat for the men who were visiting one tipi after another. Among the Crow it was the custom to give a guest food when he arrived, regardless of the time of day. The women and girls were dressed in their best: long buckskin dresses, with rows of fringes on the sides and at the hem, and heavily embroidered with colorful porcupine quills.

Everyone in camp knew that the men were planning a raid. The hunters had reported a Cheyenne camp to the southeast, between the Tongue and the Powder Rivers. "It is a large camp," the hunters said. "The trail is full of horse tracks." The scouts who had gone out to check the report agreed that a very large Cheyenne camp of about two hundred tipis was moving northward.

Several braves wanted to set out at once to raid the Cheyenne camp for horses which were needed for the next buffalo hunt. Others suggested getting together a very large war party. To the east of the Little Horn River was another large Crow camp. The men there would be glad to join the raid. But the young braves wanted to set out at once. The camp chiefs, who were older, experienced warriors, advised the young men against going, however. It was too dangerous for such a small party to attack an enemy camp as large as this one.

War and raiding parties were very important to the Crow braves. A Crow youth did not become a chief because his father was one. It was up to him to earn fame so the people would respect him, listen to him, and raise him to become a chief. Fame could only be earned through great deeds in war.

Every Crow boy knew there were four important ways to do this. Each was a great deed. We call such a deed a coup (pronounced *koo;* plural, coups, pronounced *kooz*). This is a French word and means *blow* or *stroke*. In war, or on a raid, the greatest coup was to touch an enemy with a small wand or coup stick. Every boy and warrior wanted to be the first to touch an enemy, for this was a sign that you were brave and out in front in the attack. Another great coup was to take away the bow from an enemy. A third was to steal a

CROW TERRITORY

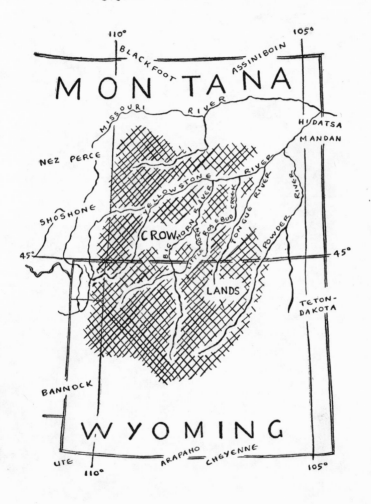

picketed horse from an enemy's camp. A fourth coup was to lead a successful war party.

To become a chief, a man had to accomplish great deeds many times. As leader or pipe carrier of a war party, a man had many opportunities to be first in striking coups. The Crow warriors did not want to kill an enemy except when they set out with the purpose of avenging the killing of a Crow. A much braver deed was to touch a sleeping Cheyenne, grab his horses or bow, and run away.

Crow boys of about fourteen, fifteen, and sixteen were usually the first to volunteer to go on a raid, for this would start them on their careers as warriors. A boy's father, uncle, or grandfather taught him to use his bow and arrows; taught him horsemanship and the rules of the warpath. But the boy himself must seek a chance to join a war party in order to count coups and so gain success and renown.

In this camp, young Eagle-claw was anxious to go on the raid which the warriors were planning. He was about fifteen. The Crow did not count people's ages as carefully as we do, but his parents thought he was about fifteen winters old. Eagle-claw was an excellent marksman and horse-man, and he had already gone on one raiding party. He begged his uncle, who was a chief, to speak for him to the leader of the war party. Eagle-claw's uncle rode off and soon returned with the good news that the boy could go, and that the leader wanted to see him at once.

Eagle-claw hastily dressed in his best leggings and shirt and tucked a war club into his belt. He would have liked to put an eagle feather or two in his hair, but he could not do this, because as yet he had no coups on his record. So he merely smoothed his hair with his hands, stood up as tall as he could, and followed his uncle out of the tipi. Both mounted their horses and rode away.

Inside the tipi, Eagle-claw's family—his father, mother, sister, and younger brother—watched the departure in silence. The Crow do not have words for either hello or good-by in their language. But Bear-cub, who was about ten win-ters old and still thought of as a child, rushed out of the tipi and ran after the horsemen. However, he remained outside the war leader's tipi when his brother went in. The planning for a raid was always done in secret. No outsiders, except a few chiefs and the medicine men, or shamans, could be present.

Now the war leader asked the shamans for advice, but the two shamans were uncertain. They wanted to pray to the spirits first and try to get the answer in a dream. The young men did not want to wait. They thought that a small war party could raid the Cheyenne camp quickly and quietly just before dawn while the enemy was asleep, capture the horses, and ride back fast.

The young hunters rode back and forth, calling on their friends to join them. The older hunters and camp chiefs tried to quiet the young braves, telling them to be careful, for the Cheyenne, like the Crow, were fearless fighters.

There were horses everywhere. Some were picketed to poles near the tipis. Some, with their forefeet hobbled, limped along as they grazed by the river behind the tipis. The horses shook their long manes and swished their long tails to chase away the swarms of flies that circled about them.

Where there were horses, there were children

and dogs. Crow youngsters were not afraid of horses. A Crow boy just tall enough to reach the short reins or grasp a horse's mane swung himself on its back. It did not matter whether the horse was picketed or hobbled, saddled or not. Tired of waiting, Younger Brother swung astride Eagle-claw's horse. Once on horseback, he grasped the reins in one hand, braced his bare brown knees against the horse's neck and helped the war leader's boy and little girl to climb up. Soon there were three or four tousled brown riders pressing with bare knees and heels against the horse's sides. Each made believe he was riding a horse of his own, galloping across the prairie after a buffalo herd. Bear-cub made believe he was on the warpath. He pressed close to the horse's neck, so the enemy would not see him as he rode to attack.

"Whooo-oo," the children yelled, as they had heard warriors shout in a war dance. "Whoo-oo." The dogs added their furious barking to the children's cries.

At the sudden noise, everyone came tumbling out of the tipis. Some of the men had grabbed their bows and arrows, although they knew that an enemy never attacked a camp in broad daylight. But you could never tell what a bold enemy brave might do. Perhaps Cheyenne scouts had seen the Crow camp and had gathered a war party together for a surprise attack.

Eagle-claw scolded his brother. "Get down, Younger Brother. You make more noise than a magpie." But the older men, holding their bows and arrows, burst into laughter. The children had fooled them. They had the Cheyenne so much on their minds and were so worried about the young braves going on the warpath that they had thought the Cheyenne had attacked first.

"How many horses did you get, Elder Brother?" An old chief teased Bear-cub by speaking to him as though he were grown up. "Get plenty. We need horses for the buffalo hunt. If you bring in plenty of horses, we'll let you lead the next war party. You can carry the pipe." This meant, "You will be the chief."

Everyone laughed as Bear-cub slid off the horse. He felt so ashamed at having disturbed the council that he hid behind his uncle. Bear-cub

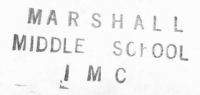

knew that his uncle was very kind and would not say anything to shame him, but he was afraid of what Eagle-claw would say to him later. As the

PEACEPIPE

men re-entered the tipi, Bear-cub headed for home.

Finally, after much talk and argument, the young Crow warriors prevailed. A small war party of eight men was organized. Eagle-claw was one of them. The war party left camp that same night, under cover of darkness. Care had to be taken that no one saw the departing warriors, for Cheyenne scouts might be lurking about. Each man left quietly on a fast horse. Since they planned to be away for only a few days, the men traveled light.

A week slipped by as everyone waited for the war party to return. All this time the camp was unusually quiet. No one spoke of the raid for fear of bringing the party bad luck. Each day hunters went out looking for antelope and deer. They wanted to have fresh meat in camp for the warriors when they returned.

Inside the tipis, the older men and boys were repairing their stone and bone tools, their bows and arrows. The women and girls worked quietly by the fires, drying meat for storage, or sewing and mending, listening for the sound of a messenger. The smaller children kept near their tipis. Considering the racket they had raised before the warriors left, the children now were strangely quiet.

It was the custom for a war party returning with loot and horses to send a fast messenger ahead to tell the camp that they were on the way back. To save time, the messenger usually stopped on a hilltop near enough to the camp to be seen.

There, waving his buckskin shirt, he let the camp know the outcome of the raid by means of signs. Men, women, and children rushed to put on their best clothes, their necklaces and feathers. Horses were rounded up and the entire camp galloped out to greet the returning party.

Then the warriors painted their faces with red and black lines and circles and formed a procession back to camp. The man who struck the first coup rode with the chief. Everyone praised him. An old man usually led his horse, repeating the great deeds the warrior had performed on this raid and on earlier ones. The old man sang:

> *"He, Fire-bear, struck an enemy.*
> *He led a war party.*
> *He killed an enemy.*
> *He was wounded.*
> *He brought twenty horses from a raid.*
> *He killed the enemy's horse.*
> *Fire-bear went on the warpath ten times."*

One morning three women and Eagle-claw's sister, Meadow-lark, went to the river to work on the buffalo hides they had put in to soak the day before. The women pulled the skins out of the water, stretched them out on the river bank, and began to scrape off the flesh with bone scrapers made from antlers. Sister was busy helping. She fetched water and splashed it over the skins to wash off the scrapings. The women had been working for some time when suddenly the girl looked up and froze where she stood, her mouth wide open, unable to utter a sound.

On a hill across the river, a Crow warrior, his face still painted with red circles and black bars, was slowly waving his shirt, moving it downward in the direction where the war party had gone. He held up his hand to show that someone had been killed, then shaped his hand into an eagle's claw.

"Eagle-claw has been killed," the girl whispered. "Older Brother is dead."

"What are you saying?" A woman reproved Meadow-lark without looking up from her scraping. "No one must ever speak of death."

"Older Brother has been killed by the Cheyenne," the girl repeated.

The three women jumped up and saw the mes-

senger repeating his signal. Defeat! The war
party had been defeated! They burst into tears
and went to meet the messenger, who ran down
to ford the river. The messenger quickly told his
story.

The war party had sent out scouts to look over
the Cheyenne camp, a camp very much like that
of the Crow. The tipis stood along a small stream.
At one end of the camp was a hill. The Cheyenne
horses grazed by the water between the hill and
the tipis. The territory was familiar to the scouts.
All seemed quiet in the early dawn, and the scouts
signaled with wolf calls for the party to advance.

While they were waiting, the men unwrapped
small packages of colored earth. They mixed these
with water and painted their faces with red and
black circles and stripes. They picketed their
horses downstream and, carrying their bows and
arrows, crawled through the grass toward the
Cheyenne camp to await the scouts' signal. At the
wolf call, they all moved silently forward.

What the scouts could not have foreseen was
that a Cheyenne boy had camped on a nearby hilltop the night before. He heard the wolf calls of

the Crow scouts and became suspicious. Hiding behind a boulder, he saw the war party creeping through the grass. He waited till they passed and then ran downhill toward his camp. A Crow warrior saw the boy and sent an arrow after him, but the boy was already too far away, too close to his camp. Meanwhile, the others were untying the hobbled horses and mounting them. The warrior's warning was too late. Shouts and voices came from the camp. The boy had given the alarm and in a few minutes the Cheyenne warriors were running toward the Crow. The Cheyenne outnumbered the small war party ten to one. There was nothing for the Crow warriors to do but set free the horses they had taken and disappear into the grass.

But Eagle-claw tried to gallop away. He had mounted a handsome Cheyenne pony and did not want to part with it. The Cheyenne closed in with a shower of arrows, killing both Eagle-claw and his horse. While the Cheyenne were chasing Eagle-claw, the other Crow spread out and hid in the tall grass. The next night, faint wolf calls led the Crow together again. Now the party was returning, not only without loot but even without their own horses. Worst of all, they had lost one of their men.

Inside their tipi, Eagle-claw's family was busy preparing a feast for his home-coming. Eagle-claw's father was finishing a shield he had made of two thick pieces of buffalo hide. The shield was round and measured almost two feet across. He had sewed a band of buckskin around the edge of the shield and tied eagle feathers to it. In the center was the design of an eagle.

Younger Brother was helping his father. He smoothed the eagle feathers lightly with a porcu-pine-tail brush. The feathers lay smooth and shiny on the platform where Eagle-claw had slept. Now the boy turned to the small horn cups that held the paint for coloring the design on the shield. He added bear grease to the cups of red and yellow earth colors and ground the mixture to make a paste. In another horn cup, Bear-cub mixed buf-falo fat with powdered charcoal to make a shiny black paint. The shield would soon be finished.

A small fire of buffalo chips burned in the fire pit in the center of the tipi. Near the fire, Eagle-claw's mother pounded thin slices of dried buffalo

meat with a stone. She looked with pleasure at
the stack of skin bags filled with dried meat and
berries. There was enough food to feast the entire

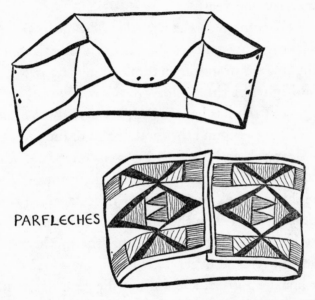

PARFLECHES

camp, she thought. They would need it all if
Eagle-claw had made his first coup. Behind the
sacks of stored food were layers of other bags.
These were also made of buffalo hide but were
folded into squares, like huge envelopes. These
parfleches held buckskins and antelope skins, buffalo robes, and hides that she had tanned. In an-

other parfleche were a pair of moccasins she had made, and in still another was her own best buckskin dress covered with elk teeth. These she would wear for the feast.

At that moment the door flap flew open. Weeping, Meadow-lark rushed over to her mother. The two wailing women tumbled in after her over the high tipi threshold.

"Your son has been killed," one of them cried.

Without a sound the mother fell to the ground.

Bear-cub and his father began to cry and wail too. They did not try to hide their grief. The neighbors shook the mother till she regained consciousness and then they helped her sit up. Swaying back and forth on the floor, the mother kept saying over and over, "My child, my son." Even in her deep grief, she did not mention his name. The Crow believed that the name of a dead person must never be mentioned, for it might disturb him on his journey to another world.

Frantic with grief, the father tore his buckskin shirt. He grabbed the bone knife he had been using and cut himself across his left hand. "This is the hand that helped you, my son, to make your bow and arrows. I give this, my flesh, to the great spirit to make your journey easier. Take pity on us, on our misery," he wailed.

Grasping a stone knife the mother gashed her face, arms, and hands. She swayed back and forth on the floor in pain and grief. Meadow-lark and Bear-cub were too young to gash their bodies or tear their clothing in mourning. They sat beside their parents and wept.

Eagle-claw had had more fun in camp than any other boy, Meadow-lark thought. He had gone to every ceremony and dance. Later the two of them had practiced the dances inside their tipi, while Bear-cub watched and criticized them. Many of the deer and antelope skins which she and her mother had just tanned and were sewing into clothing had been brought home by Eagle-claw. On the last buffalo hunt Eagle-claw had ridden far out in front with his father and all the men; and the family's share of buffalo skins and meat was as large as that of a family with two or three grown men. An older brother always helped his sister, even after he married, and always gave her the handsomest skins he shot. Now Eagle-claw was dead and Meadow-lark felt as lonely as a Crow orphan.

Bear-cub knew that his mother's brother, whom he called Elder Brother, would teach him, as he had taught Eagle-claw, to shoot, to hunt, and to make bows and arrows. But Bear-cub had learned even more just by watching Eagle-claw working or shooting at targets, or dancing and singing. No one can ever take Eagle-claw's place, Bear-cub thought. Now I shall do my best to help Father and Mother, but I am still too small and it will take many winters before I can do the things Eagle-claw did so well.

"Take all this food," Bear-cub heard Mother say to the neighbors, who crowded into the tipi. "Take it all. We won't need it now. Our loss is so great."

Bear-cub got up. He lifted the heavy sacks of dried meat, one after another, and gave them to the crowd that had gathered. The people carried away the meat sacks and the parfleches, leaving the family in an emptied tipi, to fast and grieve over the loss of a loved son and brother.

The news, the crying and commotion, set everyone in the Crow camp into frenzied action. Men and boys tumbled out of their tipis and ran for their horses, followed by the women and girls. In a short time, the men rode out of camp, leading extra horses for the defeated warriors who were still on the trail.

2

THE BUFFALO HUNT

EVERYONE in the Crow camp thought about revenge. Again the younger and more reckless men wanted action. "Let's attack the Cheyenne at once," they said.

But the older men said no. Had the younger men waited in the first place, this tragedy might not have happened. If they had taken the time to form a larger war party, they might have fought off the Cheyenne without leaving their dead behind, even though the Cheyenne far outnumbered the Crow. Now it was too late. The Cheyenne would be watching, knowing that the Crow would come seeking revenge.

Like all other young men and warriors, Eagle-claw had belonged to a club. His club was called the Hammers. Several boys, also members of the Hammers, came to see Eagle-claw's parents. Each begged: "Let me go out alone. I will kill a Cheyenne to avenge your son, so you will not have to continue fasting and mourning for him. I am not afraid to die." The grateful parents gave one of the boys, named Mud-belly, a horse, four arrows, and a large parfleche as gifts.

But new and important events were taking place. Up north of the Yellowstone River, scouts from this and another Crow camp were working together on a buffalo drive. They were driving small buffalo herds together into a larger herd for a buffalo hunt. A scout returned for more help, and said that already they had more buffalo in the herd than there were people in the camp. "This will be the biggest buffalo hunt we have ever had," he promised.

The scout was uncertain as to when the hunt would begin and told the men who guarded the camp to let no one leave. He feared that a hunter might come upon the herd and frighten it before plans for the hunt were completed, thus spoiling weeks of hard work. The Lumpwoods, a very important men's club, had been chosen to police the Crow camp, and they gave orders that no one was to leave camp without permission. If anyone disobeyed, the Lumpwoods would surely catch up with him and whip him before the entire camp, to shame him. So Mud-belly could not set out to avenge Eagle-claw.

To these Indians, the buffalo was important. It was their staff of life. Its meat and fat were their most important food. From its skin they made clothing and moccasins, tipi covers, saddles, and shields. They made containers from its skin and cooked and stored their food in them. From its horns and bones the men made spoons and bowls, knives and awls. They used its sinew to make strings for their bows and thread for sewing. Only in the mountains were there enough trees to supply wood; the wide plains were almost treeless. Therefore, dry buffalo droppings, called buffalo chips, were used for fuel to cook with and to warm the tipis. Elk, deer, antelope, mountain sheep, and bears were abundant. The Crow hunted these animals, too. They ate their meat and used their skins, but the buffalo were more useful to them than any other animals.

In those days buffalo were still plentiful. No one had counted the herds, but it is a fair guess that about sixty million head wandered over the Great Plains area. Buffalo, or bison as they are more properly called, lived over most of this continent. They spread from Pennsylvania across the continent into the Rockies. The herds wandered as far south as Georgia and northern Florida, southwest as far as the Pecos River in New Mexico, and north to what is now Alberta, Canada.

The feeding habits of the buffalo were different from those of other grazing animals. Animals of the plains, such as antelope, deer, and elk, live within a fairly limited region where they feed and roam. So a hunter, after seeing tracks of these animals by a river, knows that they will come back sooner or later, to drink. Buffalo could go longer without water than deer or antelope and were, therefore, great wanderers. Singly and in herds they moved hundreds of miles in a season. Sometimes a herd of buffalo, after passing through a region, was not seen there again for a year or more. The Indians of the plains, who depended so much on the buffalo herds, were obliged to live a wandering life, following the herds from place to place.

The Crow did no farming at all, since nearly everything they needed came from the buffalo. Tobacco, which they needed for their ceremonies, was the only plant they raised. Hunters, singly or in pairs, sometimes went after deer, elk, and antelope. Boys hunted rabbits, prairie dogs, squirrels, and birds. But the buffalo was the mainstay of these Indians.

Toward the end of the seventeenth century the Crow got horses, and then buffalo hunts became very big undertakings. Several camps often joined in the slaughter of a big buffalo herd. A camp was often moved to the place where the herd had been killed, since that was easier than carrying carcasses a long distance.

Before the Crow had horses, the large, wolf-like Crow dogs carried some of the burdens when camp was being moved. The dogs were harnessed into travois (*trah-voy*), which the women built out of long tipi poles. The upper ends of two poles were lashed to a dog's sides with rawhide thongs. The lower ends dragged on the ground as the dog trotted behind his master or mistress. At the center of the travois, a woman made a small platform out of hide and lashed a bundle of household goods to it. However, a dog could drag only thirty or forty pounds, while a horse, harnessed to a large travois, could drag a few hundred pounds and carry a woman and child on its back at the same time.

Now the Crow camp was getting ready to move for the buffalo hunt. Everyone awaited the signal from the Lumpwoods. Scouts kept the Lumpwoods posted about the herd and spread the news through the camp.

Crow children always liked the excitement of moving camp. Meadow-lark and Bear-cub especially looked forward to this, because it would give them a chance to be outdoors again with their friends and forget for a while the sorrow of their brother's death.

A Crow camp on the move was colorful and gay. There were enough horses so that the entire camp could ride. The men rode in the front, naked except for breechcloth and moccasins. Their dark well-greased bodies shone in the sun, and the eagle feathers in their hair swayed with every movement. Behind them rode the women and children on horses harnessed to the travois. The women's and girls' dresses, moccasins, and leggings were rich with porcupine-quill embroidery. Boys and girls often doubled up on one horse when there were not enough horses in the family. Little boys and girls rode behind their mothers or grandmothers. A mother tied the baby's cradleboard to the front of her saddle. When the baby cried or was hungry the mother picked it up in its cradleboard and nursed it.

Since Eagle-claw's family had only two horses

left, the father took the swifter pony and joined
the men. The mother, with the children's help,
tied their few belongings on the travois. She told
Meadow-lark to ride behind her and motioned
to Bear-cub to climb up on the travois on top of
the bundles. Bear-cub had never ridden this way
before. There had always been an extra horse for
him to ride. He looked about, hoping one of his
friends would come over and offer him a ride, but
no one came. Everyone was busy with his own
household. Bear-cub dared not hesitate long, fear-
ing his mother would know his thoughts and start
crying again about Eagle-claw. Smiling and nod-
ding to his mother, he quickly climbed up the
travois and grasped the poles firmly in his hands.
For the first time since the news about Eagle-claw
had reached them, the mother and Meadow-lark
smiled too.

"We'll trade some buffalo robes after the hunt
for a few horses, son," the mother promised.
"And you may have the swiftest of them for your
own."

The spot chosen for the new camp was a half
day's ride away. It was at the edge of a coulee

(*koo-lee*), a steep-walled valley. This was a place where a river had once tumbled in a majestic waterfall. Long ago the river's course had been changed, and now green grass filled the river valley. A path led directly to the cliff of the old waterfall. The hunters planned to drive the buffalo herd over this cliff. As the animals fell over the cliff, they would be killed. The camp was set up nearby.

Now everyone began to dismount. The women chose places on the prairie to set up their tipis. They took the loads off the travois and untied the travois poles from the saddles. The boys helped hobble the horses and turned them loose to graze.

It did not take the women very long to set up the tipis. Each woman tied together three of the longest poles a foot or two from their tops with heavy rawhide thongs. These poles were over twenty feet long. Since the Crow had no ladders, the woman laid the poles on the ground, slipped the tipi cover over the poles, and tied the narrow neck of the cover to the rawhide thongs. Then she raised and spread the three poles, till the tipi cover was tight, and pressed the sharpened ends of the poles into the ground. Working from the inside, she placed long thin poles between the first three to give the tipi more support. These smaller poles were pushed through the top of the tipi cover and stuck into the ground, forming a large circle. She then pushed poles through the two smoke flaps at the top of the tipi, so they could be closed at night. Over the opening into the tipi, she put a buffalo robe.

Inside their tipi, Meadow-lark and Bear-cub were busy tearing out the grass and digging up the sagebrush from the tipi floor. They stamped the earth floor down till it was smooth. Using a sharpened buffalo rib, Meadow-lark dug a small pit for the fire. Bear-cub went out and brought in dry buffalo chips and made a small pile of them in the fireplace. He gathered another pile of chips and put it outside the tipi for future use.

Everyone helped carry the household goods into the tipi. The back of the tipi was reserved for the parents. Robes were laid on the floor, making a soft bed. In front of the bed, the mother stretched a robe between two poles to make a separate compartment. Meadow-lark would sleep on one side of the tipi, and her belongings and robe were placed there to make a bed. Bear-cub would sleep on the other side of the tipi, so his possessions and robe were placed there. In between the sleeping places, they piled the empty parfleches and sacks.

Meanwhile, the large herd of over a thousand buffalo was grazing peacefully, about fifty miles to the north. A buffalo herd covered only a few miles a day, as it fed. The bulls grazed on the outer lines of the herd while the cows and calves remained in the center. From a distance, the heavy bulls with their large, blunt, shaggy heads seemed to stand still. The thick, long, almost black hair on their heads and necks waved in the breeze. The rest of the animal behind the heavy, hairy head and hump looked almost slender with its lighter fur and short, stubby tail. The bulls were always on guard. They could see very little with their small eyes, but their sense of smell and their hearing were exceptionally good. That is why hunters had to move carefully while tracking the herd. The least noise might frighten the bulls and start a stampede.

A buffalo herd in a stampede was a terror. The frightened animals rushed blindly onward, galloping at ten miles an hour and more, hour after hour. Some bulls weighed nearly a ton, and when they were stampeding they plowed through anything in their path. They bent their heads low, relying on their sharp horns to clear the way. Very few things could withstand this onrush. The buffalo flattened trees and bushes in the frenzy of the stampede and tore up the prairie with their sharp hoofs. A man caught in their path was doomed to certain death.

The buffalo cow was much smaller than the bull, weighing between eight hundred and a thousand pounds. It, too, had horns, but they were shorter and thinner. Buffalo calves looked very much like our calves, except that they were tawny and heavier. Their necks and legs were shorter, and their heads blunter. Like our calves, they were frisky little animals, and snuggled right under their mothers as they nursed.

As they grazed, the bulls raised their heads from time to time, looked about with their little, dull eyes, and sniffed the air. The feeding buffalo

swished their tails furiously, trying to drive off
the swarms of flies and other insects. As the heat
of the day increased, the heavy coats of the buffalo

BUFFALO COW
AND CALF

got hotter and hotter and the insects became un-
bearable. One by one, the huge bulls bent their
forelegs to a kneeling position and rolled over on
their sides. Kicking and rolling from side to side,
they rubbed the prairie dust into their burning

hides. If there had been damp ground or water nearby, the rolling buffalo would soon have churned it into mud. Rolling in the mud, the buffalo would have been covered with the cooling mud plaster.

Now and then a flock of magpies came to the buffalo's aid. These birds liked to perch on the buffalo and feed on the insects stuck in its hair.

When all was ready for the drive, the hunters rode out onto the prairie and took their positions along the side of the dry river valley, in accordance with orders from the Lumpwoods. Usually, the members of other men's clubs in camp, the Foxes, the Big Dogs, and the Muddy Hands, would not be ordered about by a Lumpwood, but on a buffalo hunt everyone worked together. Even when grazing peacefully, the buffalo hated the smell of horses and would lunge at a horse that came close. So the Crow horsemen kept well out of the herd's path, forming a long line behind the herd and on either side of it. The open path for the buffalo led toward the cliff and the coulee below.

Now the chief of the Lumpwoods raised his

arm and waved his spear. This was the signal.
Together the hunters shouted "Whoo-oo, whooo-
oo." In a flash, the bulls raised their shaggy heads,
listened, and were off. The stampede had begun!
The earth shook as thousands of hoofs hit the
ground.

Keeping their distance, the men waved buckskins and spears, shouting at the top of their lungs.
Boys rode behind their fathers, waving buckskins
and shouting too. The herd had to be kept moving in the direction of the coulee.

Soon the women and children waiting on the
high ground above the valley, with Meadow-lark
and Bear-cub among them, saw the approaching
herd—a brown mass plunging down the narrow
valley. Carried away with excitement, they, too,
yelled "Whooo-oo," till they were out of breath.
The herd passed them by, leaving behind a heavy
cloud of dust. As the dust cleared, the people saw
that the prairie had been torn up as though with
a giant shovel.

Now the stampeding herd reached the cliff
with the coulee about fifty feet below. As the buffalo came galloping to the cliff, they plunged or

were pushed to their death. For a while the crying of the buffalo in the coulee filled everyone's
ears. When the last buffalo went over the cliff,

the men dismounted and began to finish off the
struggling, wounded animals with their spears and
their bows and arrows. Later, the owners of the
arrows would claim the buffalo they shot for
themselves.

From the place where the women and children

stood watching, they saw the last buffalo disappear over the cliff. The prairie became silent. The cloud of dust had lifted and the sky was cloudless and clear. Bear-cub looked up at his mother in wonder. Except for the wide trail below them, scooped out by thousands of hoofs, the stampeding herd might have been only a vision. The buffalo drive was over.

3

THE FEAST

THE men had already begun their work in the coulee when the women and girls joined them. They were skinning and cutting up the buffalo carcasses. Over a thousand buffalo had been killed. Since the hunt had been a joint undertaking, the buffalo would be divided equally among the Crow families from the two camps. There were about three hundred tipis in the two camps, so there would be several buffalo for each—enough food for every family for a month or two, and plenty of work for the women and girls who would dry the meat and tan the hides.

Each tried to choose sleek animals with un-damaged hides. Even though the bulls had more meat on them, cows were preferred, because their meat was more fatty and tender. The Crow liked meat with a good deal of fat. The women set to work with zeal. In their practiced hands the bone knives slashed speedily into the layers of fat, sepa-rating the skin from the meat. The few women who had steel knives worked even faster and could do more work. The men and boys pulled off the hides as the women and girls cut.

Despite their skill, however, skinning and cut-ting were slow work. But the Crow planned to spend a long time at this camp, for it would take many days to dry the meat and tan the skins. That was why a camp usually moved to the place where the buffalo were killed. It was easier to prepare the meat and skins on the spot than to carry them a long distance. Meat on the hot prairie spoils very quickly. It had to be cut up and dried as fast as possible, to keep it from spoiling. Hides, on the other hand, if soaked and scraped, could be worked at a later time when the women were not so busy.

The Crow liked to move to a new camp site, where the grounds were not littered and dusty and the horses had fresh grazing. The horses, like the people, lived off the land. They fed pretty well during the spring, summer, and fall, and managed to survive the snowy winters, foraging for themselves in sheltered valleys. The Crow had not yet learned to gather in hay and provide fodder for the horses.

Right now the coulee and camp smelled like a slaughterhouse. Coyotes were lurking in the tall grass, attracted by the smell of fresh meat, but wary of the moving people. Vultures were already circling overhead, and the boys chased them with long whips. Flies swarmed everywhere, annoying the sweating Indians. But the men and women kept on working.

Already several women had stuck poles into

the ground and put up several long twisted rawhide lines between the poles. On these lines the children hung slices of fresh meat to dry. The women rolled up the fresh hides and carried them to the water. They piled the buffalo heads and legs near the tipis to dry. These would get their attention later, when the rush of skinning and hanging the meat up to dry was over.

The women also brought up skin bags filled with warm buffalo blood for the children to drink. The children were glad to drink it, for they were hungry, having eaten very little during the day. Men and women also drank the nourishing blood.

As the sun was setting, the tired people clambered out of the coulee and headed for their tipis to eat and rest. Inside their tipi, Bear-cub's father quickly put a pointed stick into a small grooved board. As he twirled the stick in his hands, it produced heat, and the dry buffalo chips and grass under the small board began to smolder and smoke. As Bear-cub blew on them, the sparks soon burst into flame, and they had a small fire going. The dry buffalo chips burned quickly, heating the stones underneath. Bear-cub's mother and

Meadow-lark pulled the stones out and put fresh meat on them to roast.

In the center of the camp, some of the women had built a large fire and put in a pile of rounded stones, which the children had gathered in the coulee, to heat. Near the fire, the women dug a large pit. When finished, it was about five feet square and three feet deep. After sweeping the pit clean and lining it with grass, the women put a layer of hot stones on the grass and a layer of meat on top of the stones. Then they put in another layer of grass, a layer of hot stones, and a layer of meat on top. They covered the meat with more hot stones and grass and poured water over them. Then the pit was covered with a buffalo skin and dirt was piled on top of it, so the steam would not escape. The meat inside the pit would steam all night and all the next day and then would be ready for the feast.

The sun set. All at once it grew dark and cold on the prairie, and everyone retired to the tipis. In the dark the fires glowed red through the tipi covers and the tipis looked like huge dunce caps set about the plain. Even the dogs, gorged with meat, were tired and lay close to the tipis.

The weary men, women, and children sat down on their robes by the fires and ate the juicy fresh buffalo meat and fat. It had been a good hunt, but everyone was too tired to talk about it. The children would have liked to ask their fathers about the scouting for the herd, but their stomachs were full and their eyes were shutting, despite their best efforts to keep awake. So one by one, the children stretched out on the soft robes and fell asleep by the fires. Soon the grownups lay down, covered themselves with their robes, and went to sleep.

Bear-cub and Meadow-lark ate their fill of the juicy steaks their mother had prepared, but their parents ate only a few mouthfuls and drank some of the buffalo blood. They were thinking of Eagle-claw and how much he would have enjoyed this successful buffalo hunt.

At dawn the women and girls were back in the coulee, cutting up buffalo carcasses. By midday the entire camp was full of long lines of drying meat. Little boys and girls chased the flies and magpies away from the meat with long whips and sticks. As they tired, the children ran into their tipis to eat more of the juicy slices of steak their mothers had started to roast before they left to finish the skinning. The children had stuffed themselves the night before, but fresh meat was a treat and they could never get enough of it. The men were still sleeping or resting in the tipis, so the children tiptoed in and out quietly.

When they had finished cutting up the meat, the women went down to the water, where they had left the hides. They dammed off a little area near the bank of the stream, and put the hides in to soak.

Other women and girls, in the meantime, were busy with the drying racks. In the clear air of the prairie, meat dries quickly. Some of the thin slices they had hung up the day before were already dry. Part of this well-dried meat the women put away in skin bags. This jerked meat would be used first. They now set about making pemmican from the rest.

The women and girls built fires nearby and put slices of the dried meat on sticks to toast over the fire. After the slices had toasted till they were crisp, the women took them off the sticks, placed them on a thick piece of hide, and pounded them with a stone hammer. Then they put the sweet marrow from the buffalo bones and some fat into a sack made of heavy hide, added water, and put in heated stones. As the mixture began to boil, the melted fat rose to the surface. The girls skimmed the fat off with horn spoons, poured it over the pounded meat and let it cool. This was pemmican.

The women packed the pemmican into skin bags, where it would keep without spoiling for a year or more. Men and boys took pemmican along when they went hunting or on the warpath. They bit off a piece and chewed it as they marched. At home, children chewed pemmican when they were hungry between meals. For a meal or feast the women boiled the pemmican, adding dried berries or wild plums to make a tasty dish.

Nothing pleased a Crow woman more than to have all the skin bags she owned full of pemmican and dried meat—food enough to last for months. Making the pemmican took a long time, and the women had to keep fires burning by the drying lines. Day after day the camp would resound with the pounding of the meat. It was fun for the women and girls, who worked in groups, talking, gossiping, laughing, and singing as they worked.

But now the second day after the buffalo hunt was drawing to a close. During the day, as people passed the tightly covered pit where the buffalo meat was steaming, they could not see even a wisp of steam escaping. In the late afternoon, everyone hurried to the tipis to get dressed for the feast. Husband and wife combed each other's long hair with brushes of porcupine quills, smoothed it with grease, and braided it carefully. The men put on their embroidered buckskin shirts and leggings, new moccasins, and all the necklaces and earrings they owned. They tied eagle feathers in their black hair. In addition, each man took his shield and coup stick with him. Some of the men who were chiefs in the Crow military clubs carried poles or staffs with otter skins and feathers wound on them. These staffs were their sign of authority. The leaders of the four important clubs, the Lumpwoods, the Foxes, the Big Dogs, and Muddy Hands, came to the feast with all the trappings of their offices.

The women, too, dressed up in their best long buckskin dresses, decorated with elk teeth and

EAGLE CLAW NECKLACE

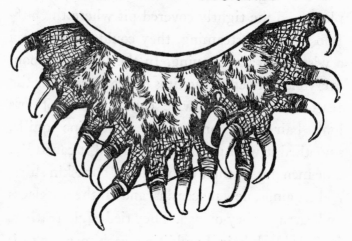

quill embroidery. The girls dressed exactly like their mothers. The boys dressed like their fathers in embroidered shirts and leggings.

When they finished dressing, the people did not go out of their tipis. They waited patiently till the camp criers, also dressed in their best and carrying staffs, their faces painted with black and red stripes, knocked on the tipis, calling everyone to come to the feast. The people, bringing robes to sit on, began to fill the square near the pit. Men sat with the other members of their club. Their wives and small children were behind them. Older boys who belonged to the Hammers sat together too. The older girls sat quietly with their mothers. The children talked in low tones, asking their mothers to explain what each group was doing, for the Mountain Crow also sat with their clubs, which were similar to those of the River Crow.

Bear-cub and Meadow-lark sat down with a neighbor's family. Their parents could not come to the feast, because they were in mourning.

To the Crow a feast meant not just eating good food, but enjoying food, dancing, singing, and games, too. While it was still light enough, the chiefs suggested that the women play a game of shinny. Shinny was a ball game which women usually played, although sometimes men played it against women. The chiefs now suggested that the Mountain Crow women play against the River Crow women. At each end of a large square the men placed robes. These were the goals. A chief's wife brought out a small buckskin ball, the size of a handball, stuffed with buffalo hair.

A group of Mountain women and girls lined up in the center of the field, facing their goal. Opposite them a group of River Crow women and girls lined up, facing theirs. Each woman had in her hand a long stick which was slightly curved and flattened at the end, like our field-hockey sticks.

A chief tossed the ball into the air. Each team had to try to get the ball through the line of opponents to its own goal. There were many excellent runners among the women, and they played a fast game. A River Crow girl almost reached the goal, but several Mountain Crow girls caught up with her and blocked her. All of them fell to the ground in a heap, pushing each other, while the spectators laughed. But a Mountain Crow got the ball away and turned toward her goal, with the River Crow hot in pursuit.

Everyone yelled and encouraged his team, although no one could be understood in the uproar.

It was getting dark and the players kept losing

the ball in the tall grass, so the game was called off, to be continued the following day.

In the meantime, the women who were not playing shinny brought out a stiff buffalo hide. They had looped a twisted rawhide rope through the ends of it. Men and women formed a circle around the hide and lifted it together, holding it taut. The neighbor with whom Meadow-lark sat told her to challenge a boy to the game. Meadow-lark looked all over for Mud-belly. He had been Eagle-claw's best friend and she did not feel as shy with him as she felt with the other boys. But Mud-belly could not be found. His parents said he had not been home for several days and they were anxious about him. Everyone was waiting for the game to begin, so Meadow-lark selected another boy. Both of them stepped onto the hide. As the people lifted the hide, Meadow-lark tried to push the boy off. Four times the hide was lifted. Finally, she managed to push him off and remain standing herself, on the lifted hide. Meadow-lark had won, and everyone shouted approval.

Several other girls and the boys whom they

challenged had a chance to compete, amid laughter and shouts.

It was now time to eat. When everyone was seated, the chiefs' wives got up and removed the

cover from the pit. Steam shot up and with it the savory smell of freshly steamed beef. Although the Crow men and boys had been eating all day, they felt hungry all over again. The women scraped away the grass, pulled out the stones, and passed around huge chunks of meat to the men.

The men cut up the chunks for themselves and their families. Everyone ate quickly, and soon the pit was empty. The women wrapped some of the leftover meat in buckskins to take home.

The Lumpwood men now got up to dance. They moved slowly past the fire in single file, shaking their rattles and stamping—heel and toe —in rhythm. The men felt sluggish with all the food they had eaten, and some of them would have liked to sit down. But the club chiefs kept reaching out with their staffs, touching the laggards on the shoulders. Every man had to dance. Even the Hammers got up and did a short dance.

Overhead stretched the vast sky. To the Crow, the dome of the sky, filled with twinkling stars, was like a tremendous tipi stretched over the entire earth. The bright sickle of the moon was like an opening in the tipi—the smoke hole you always saw as you looked up in your own home. This was an opening into another world, the world of spirits.

Since childhood they had all been told legends about the sun and the stars. Each boy and girl recalled, as he or she looked up at the Big Dipper, the story of how it came to be.

Once the seven stars in the Big Dipper were seven boys who lived on earth. But these seven boys wanted to live forever. "What shall we turn into to live forever?" they asked one another.

"Let us be the earth," one said.

"No, that won't do," said another. "The earth caves in."

"Let us be trees then."

"No, that won't do. Trees are chopped down."

"Then we'll turn into stones," suggested another boy.

"No, no. Stones are flaked to make arrows and hammers."

"How about turning into mountains?"

"No, mountains wash away and crumble."

"Let us turn into stars."

They all agreed to that. "Some stars fall down," said one of the boys, "but we won't. We'll keep together and help each other stay up."

And that is how the Big Dipper was formed and it has remained up above ever since.

"Whoo—oo, whoo-oo!" The feasting crowd suddenly heard a wolf call above the noise of the rattles and dancing. Someone was coming. The Hammers were the first to jump up, quickly followed by Bear-cub and Meadow-lark. Mud-belly had been missing from the camp ever since the buffalo hunt began, and the boys suspected that he had gone to the Cheyenne camp to avenge Eagle-claw. A horseman, leading a pony, now came into the firelight. It was Mud-belly.

He had left quietly at sunset three days before, not sure whether he would return alive. He had traveled fast all night in search of the Cheyenne camp. At last, on the following day, he saw their horses. A boy was watching them. Mud-belly crawled up to the boy, touched him with his coup stick, then hit him with his war club, and scalped him.

The chief of the Hammers lifted the scalp from Mud-belly's saddle for everyone to see. He tied the scalp to the end of a club staff and gave it to Meadow-lark, who led the parade around the fire with it. Bear-cub and all the men, women, and children joined them, singing:

"Alone he went to the enemy.
He counted coup.
He killed.
He avenged his brother."

One of the camp criers carried the good news to Eagle-claw's parents. They had not come to the feast, since people in mourning did not attend festivities and dances. The parents quickly put on their very best clothes, combed their hair, and rushed to the feast. Bear-cub took the reins of Mud-belly's horse, as Eagle-claw's parents joined in with the singing and dancing. Their son had been avenged!

4

A CROW BOY'S DAY

For the next few days the hunters stayed near
the camp, and scouts were posted in nearby hills.
But no Cheyenne warriors came seeking revenge.
The old men knew that sooner or later the Cheyenne would come. In the meanwhile, everything
went on as usual and there was plenty for everyone to do. Even the children were not idle.

A Crow boy's day was a busy day. A boy had to prepare for the life of a hunter and warrior—a hard life that called for a strong body, skill, and independence. He had to become a good hunter in order to make a living, but no one told him where and when to hunt. That he had to decide for himself, except when a big buffalo hunt was taking place. Then everyone had to follow the rules, so as not to disturb the herd and spoil the hunt for everyone else. At other times a hunter was free to hunt alone if he chose.

The Crow admired courage and generosity above everything, so each boy wanted to be brave and generous. The best way to show courage was to go on the warpath and face the enemy bravely. That is why boys were anxious to go to war. The best way for a young warrior to show generosity was to give away the loot for which he had risked his life. That, too, each boy wanted to do.

Bear-cub's childhood had been like that of every little boy in camp. When very young, he played with other little boys and girls, and the men paid no more attention to him than they did to the girls. Everyone was kind to children and

helped them, but the men did not show any par-
ticular interest in very little boys. Grandfather
had made toy horses, deer, and antelope out of
wood, bone, and skins for Bear-cub, while Grandmother made dolls and tipis for Meadow-lark.
Bear-cub had played house with the other little
boys and girls and watched the older children ride
horseback, shoot their bows and arrows, and play
their games.

Because a boy expected to spend so much of his
time away from home, he had few household
duties. Now that Bear-cub was older, all he had
to do on waking was to fold his sleeping robe. If
he felt like going out immediately, he put his
hand into the skin bag containing the pemmican,
filled a small pouch with it, tied the pouch to his
belt, picked up his bow and arrows and his lasso,
and left the tipi. If he felt hungry, he chewed
on a piece of pemmican.

Bear-cub left the tipi early one day several
weeks after the feast. In this warm weather he
wore, like the rest of the boys, only a breechcloth
and moccasins. The breechcloth was a wide piece
of buckskin tucked between his legs and looped

front and back over a belt, with the ends hanging loose. His mother had embroidered the ends of the breechcloth and the tops of his moccasins with porcupine quills.

Bear-cub did not have to go very far by himself. His friends came out of their tipis, looked up at the sky and, satisfied that all was well, joined him. Yesterday they had planned just where they were going today. Bear-cub's mother had kept her promise. She had given him the first horse she received in trade—for a buffalo robe which she and Meadow-lark had tanned and embroidered right after the buffalo hunt.

As soon as the boys were out of sight of the camp, two of them, who were to act as scouts for the day, disappeared behind a clump of sagebrush. The rest went to lasso their horses. The boys still remembered the many weary hours they had spent lassoing a tree stump, pretending it was a horse. When a boy dropped his rawhide loop over the stump everyone praised him, as though he had lassoed a real horse. With the skill learned from all that practice, they now lassoed their horses quickly. No one had bothered about a saddle; they all rode bareback.

The boys mounted their horses and raced away. At first they rode abreast. Then they broke into two groups and had a relay race. They pointed their arrows at each other; they dodged and twisted from side to side. Sometimes a boy, holding the horse by the neck, would ride under its belly. This practice would come in handy later when they were on the warpath and under enemy fire.

Tired and sweaty, Bear-cub and his companions lay down to rest and cool off. Holding the long reins, they let the horses graze. Their scouts had not yet returned. One boy took out a piece of pemmican to chew and offered the pouch to the others. But they all had their own pouches of pemmican. They chewed in silence, enjoying their rest in the cool grass.

There was a sudden movement in the grass and instantly they were all on the alert. They quickly picked up their bows and readied their arrows. The movement in the grass could be anything; it could be any of the small game they were always hunting—a rabbit, prairie dog, chipmunk, or squirrel. But it could also be an enemy scout!

As they had seen the men do when hunting deer or elk, the boys stopped talking and used signs instead, pointing with their lips and chins. They were sure the movement had not been made by one of their own scouts, because he would have called to them, imitating the sharp howl of a wolf.

The grass moved again and now a rabbit leaped up and disappeared. Bear-cub aimed. His arrow flew. "I got it," he whispered. The others rushed to see.

It was a large rabbit. While the others watched, Bear-cub took out his knife and opened a vein in the rabbit's neck. He laid the rabbit with its head downhill so it would bleed freely, as he had seen his father bleed deer. While the rabbit bled, Bear-cub began to skin it. He was careful not to damage the skin, so his mother would be able to use it. When he had removed the skin, he cut up the rabbit, threw away the entrails, and wrapped the meat carefully in the skin. He hung the bundle of meat on a tree in the shade.

Since the afternoon was hot, the boys mounted

their horses again and raced to the river for a swim. They picketed their horses and jumped in with their breechcloths on. A wet breechcloth would keep a boy cool for the rest of the afternoon. Their shoulder-length hair became tangled as they dived. They shook it away from their faces and raced each other across the stream.

In a little cove by the river bank nearby, several men had built a sweat lodge. It was a low rounded hut made of willow branches and covered with two buffalo robes. The narrow opening was just big enough to let a man crawl in. The men had built a fire outside the sweat lodge and heated stones in it. They had piled the hot stones inside the sweat lodge and poured water over the stones. The steam from the hot stones made a steam bath for the men inside, and they must stand the heat as long as they could. Now, as the boys watched, the men dashed out and dived into the river.

Bear-cub and the others knew what that meant. "I heard Older Brother say that this raid will be against the Dakota," one boy said softly.

It was the custom among the Crow, as among all the Plains Indians, to purify themselves in a sweat bath before going to war. In addition to the sweat bath, the men usually fasted, too.

On the evening before they left for the enemy camp, the men also held a secret dance in the tipi where their club met. They sang their songs and danced to please the spirits. Then, they believed, the spirits would help to make the raid a success. Each man who was going on the raid enacted in his dance just what he planned to do on the raid. He would creep into the enemy's camp. He would win his first coup by touching a sleeping enemy with his coup stick. Then he would count another coup on a picketed horse. Next he would lasso several horses, mount one, and turn swiftly homeward. Each man believed that the spirit which watched over him would now know just what he wanted and help him get it.

To gain success and renown as a warrior, a young brave believed he needed guidance from a special power. He could get this power only from the spirits. The Crow believed that the spirits lived all about them—in rocks, in trees, in the water, as well as inside animals and men. The sun, the moon, the stars, lightning, and thunder had special powers too. A boy hoped to get one of these powers to take care of him and help him. The Crow were sure that the spirits pitied a man when he was in great misery. When he was hungry and in pain the spirits would give him special power.

The best way for a boy to reach the spirits was to go off alone to some mountaintop to fast and pray. The Crow called this going in search of a vision. A boy usually stayed away from home four days, since the Crow considered four a lucky number.

Alone on the mountaintop, cold and exhausted from his fasting, the boy would fall asleep. Whatever he dreamed was his vision. He then told it to his father or to the chiefs and the camp shaman. They, in turn, told the boy what his dream meant and what the spirit wanted him to do.

Having had a vision, a boy was anxious to try out his new power. There were always several boys in every Crow camp who were eager to go on the warpath.

"Do you know who is going on this raid?" Bear-cub whispered.

"I heard talk," another boy replied. "I asked my father to speak to their chief about taking me, but no one has invited me yet. It may be that boys will not be taken this time."

Although most of these boys were only thirteen or fourteen, several of them had already had their first vision. Bear-cub remembered how Eagle-claw had fasted on the mountain and had had his vision. He now told it to the boys.

Eagle-claw had fasted all day and had wandered about on the hilltop. The sun was burning hot and he was thirsty, but he did not dare go down to get a drink. The night was cold and windy. He shivered with hunger and cold, and pressed against an overhanging ledge which acted as a windbreak. He fasted the next day, too. The sun burned hot during the day and the night again was very cold. Eagle-claw was hungry and thirsty, yet he did not leave his post.

On the third day, as the sun was setting, Eagle-claw chopped off the tip of his little finger and held his hand up to the sky, crying with the pain.

"I am poor," he said. "Have pity on me. Give me something. Give me a horse. May I become a chief! May I be rich!"

The blood kept spurting from his finger. He fell to the ground, pressing his fist hard against his chest to lessen the throbbing pain. He lay there without moving, feeling the blood oozing out and wetting his shirt. Finally he dozed off and dreamed.

"In my vision, there was a storm coming." Bear-cub had listened breathlessly as Eagle-claw told the story to their father. "I wanted to look for shelter. As I was getting up, a bird came out of the clouds toward me. He was a large bird. He descended noiselessly, but lightning came from his eyes. He sat down on the ground. Smoke was coming from him. The storm was raging all around. Hailstones were falling, but they touched neither the bird nor me. There was a dry circle around us, where the bird and I sat. The bird spoke. He said: 'Whatever you ask for, I will do it for you. I live up in the sky and am going to take care of you. I am going to adopt you. That is why I came down.'

"Then the bird spread its wings, flew off and disappeared upward into the dark. I lay thinking of my vision. The hailstones kept falling, and they repeated what the bird had said. 'Whatever you ask for, I will do it for you.' "

When the chiefs heard Eagle-claw's vision, they agreed that the bird was an eagle and that Eagle-claw would have its power.

His father's relatives made new buckskin clothing for Eagle-claw and embroidered the new clothes with red porcupine quills. His father's brothers traded for a set of eagle claws and made a necklace for the boy. When the women finished their sewing, they took down the tipi. With charcoal the boy drew on a piece of buckskin a design showing the shape of the eagle he had seen. The women enlarged this design on the tipi cover and painted it with earth colors—red, yellow, and black.

Eagle-claw rested in the tipi for a few days, then joined a war party. He believed firmly in his vision and was confident of success, but since this was his first time on the warpath, the leader told

him to remain hidden in the grass and watch what the others did. Eagle-claw had to obey.

When Bear-cub finished the story of Eagle-claw and his vision, another boy told about his own experience. Like Eagle-claw, he had fasted and had cut off a finger joint. Then he had seen his vision.

"I felt weak from hunger and pain and shut my eyes," he began. "Suddenly I saw a hunter on a horse. He was the handsomest man I have ever seen. He wore embroidered buckskins. His saddle and saddlebags were also embroidered with porcupine quills. His braids almost touched the ground and his hair shone in the sun. The rider did not dismount when he saw me. His horse stopped near me and the rider said, 'Ask me for anything and I will give it to you, my son.' I awoke. The sun was shining in my eyes. So I got up and ran home."

The boy told how his parents helped him get a suit like the one the rider wore in his vision, and how he himself had showed the women the design on the rider's clothing, saddle, and saddlebags. They had carried out this design in making the boy his clothes, saddle, and saddlebags. "But so far," he told the others, "I have had no chance to go on the warpath. When I am permitted to go, I shall be successful, because the rider of my vision will help me."

All the others joined in, telling of elk, antelope, beavers, bears, and birds that had appeared in visions. Each vision promised help to the dreamer, and sometimes he was given rules to obey. "Don't eat heart or liver," one boy was warned.

"Older Brother saw a buffalo in his vision," another boy said. "The buffalo bull was mighty, but gray."

The chiefs believed this meant that the boy would live to a ripe old age. The old buffalo was leading the herd, which meant the boy would become a great leader. The buffalo let the boy mount him, as though he were a horse, and said, "Call me and I will help you." As the boy grew up, he took the lead on buffalo hunts. He charged after the buffalo and shouted, "Here I come. I am Gray Buffalo." This, he felt sure, gave him strong power over the buffalo he hunted.

The gray buffalo gave a rule to the boy. "Never eat buffalo tongue." Although the Crow thought the tongue the tastiest part of the buffalo, the boy never ate it again.

Talking of visions, the boys had almost forgotten the two scouts. Now they heard wolf calls and answered them. The two scouts came running.

"There are rabbits everywhere," they reported. "Come! This will be a big rabbit hunt."

The boys left their picketed horses, took their bows and arrows, and followed the scouts. There were many rabbits, and soon each of the boys had shot one or two.

One rabbit leaped right in front of the boys, then dashed away. "That rabbit acts crazy," Bear-cub said.

The boys stopped running after rabbits and lay down quietly in the grass. Soon the rabbit returned, its nose twitching, smelling danger. It leaped about but then, seeing no enemies, it turned toward its burrow. Bear-cub jumped up and in a flash the rabbit again leaped past him and away.

There were three tiny baby rabbits in the burrow. One by one, the boys looked into the burrow at the baby rabbits, but no one touched them.

"We must not shoot that rabbit," the boys agreed. They had often heard their fathers say that a hunter must never shoot a doe with a fawn. "These little rabbits will die without their mother. We must not shoot her. We have enough meat for the feast."

Carrying their game, the boys returned to the river to cool off. They bled, skinned, and cut up the rabbits they had bagged. Again they lay down in the grass by the river bank, where the willows grew. The boys cut the green willow twigs and whipped them about on the grass.

Bear-cub thought, as he peeled the bark off a twig, about how he had made snow-snakes last winter. He had peeled the bark off a willow shoot. Then he had twisted the bark around the stick in a spiral design and held the stick over the fire till the stick was covered with soot. When he unwound the bark, he had a design in black and white on the stick. He then painted the white patches with red and yellow, so everyone would easily recognize his stick. He had made several such snow-snakes.

In winter, when snow covered the ground, he played snow-snake with the other boys. Each boy hurled his stick with an underhand pitch so that

it glided along the snow. One boy's stick glided farther than all the others. He won all the sticks the other boys threw, including Bear-cub's. The winner picked three of the best sticks for himself and gave the rest to his friends.

"Remember the snow-snake games we had?" Bear-cub asked his friends.

They did remember, but they thought sledding was more fun. The boys had covered ten buffalo ribs with rawhide. The curved part of the ribs made the front part of the sled. Two of the boys seated themselves in the sled and started it downhill.

Mud-belly had asked the boys to let him have the sled, so he could take a ride with a girl he liked. The boys lent him their sled. He seated the girl comfortably in it, then got in himself, and tucked his robe about the girl, so she would keep warm. The boys watched the couple going downhill several times and then asked to have their sled back. But Mud-belly was enjoying himself and refused to give it up. When next he started downhill, the boys ran after the sled and spilled Mud-belly and the girl into a snowdrift. The boys burst out laughing as they recalled this.

"Let's have a shooting game," Bear-cub said, "before we swim."

Almost every day when they met, the boys practiced shooting. They propped up a target made of grass against a tree stump. Each shot at it in turn, to see whose arrows would hit the center most often. Ever since Eagle-claw's death, Bear-cub had practiced longer than the other boys. He wanted to become as good a marksman as his brother had been.

Now each boy, as his turn came, stood up on the line which measured the distance from the grass target. He took careful aim and let his arrow fly.

"Good, good," his friends encouraged him, if he bettered his earlier shots. If he did not, they said, "Try again. You will have better luck."

The sun was slowly moving toward the horizon. "Time for the meeting," one of the boys said. They mounted their horses, and each rode away to his own tipi.

This meeting was to be no ordinary boys' feast, but a very special occasion. The younger boys had been invited by several older ones in the camp to join the boys' club, the Hammers. Each was asked to bring some meat for the feast. Bear-cub dressed in his best buckskins and put a turkey feather in his hair. All the boys had dressed up for the occasion, as they had seen the men do when they went to their club meetings. Soon the friends met again, each carrying meat for the feast. They walked toward the field where the Hammers were to hold the meeting, put the meat in a pile on a buffalo hide, and sat down next to the older boys who had asked them to come.

The four chiefs of the club, carrying their staffs of office decorated with feathers and otter skins, got the fire going and began to roast the fresh meat. They asked the old members, who had had visions, to dance and sing. Each sang a song about his vision and danced—heel and toe— a buffalo dance or an eagle dance, a bear dance or the dance of the Thunderbird. The steps of the dance imitated the walk of the bear or buffalo, the flight of the eagle, or the imaginary flight of the Thunderbird. Since each boy in his performance was repeating what he had seen in his dream, everyone watched and listened carefully and quietly, so the spirits would not be offended.

The dances and songs lasted a long time. The smell of the roasting meat made Bear-cub very hungry, but he waited patiently. At last the danc-

ing and singing were over and the four club chiefs passed the roasted meat around.

Mud-belly, who had invited Bear-cub to the feast, told him that he and his friends should come again tomorrow night. They would then meet the four new chiefs, whom the old club members had chosen. Each boy was free to choose one of the four as his leader. Mud-belly further explained that each leader would bring a peace pipe with him. The leader and his new followers would each take a few puffs to bind their friendship, as the men did in their clubs. Then they would go to the new leader's tipi for a feast. The leader's father gave this feast to honor his son.

Bear-cub was very happy that he had at last joined the Hammers, even though he was the youngest member. Whenever men went to war, they usually invited one or two Hammer members to come along to learn about the ways of the warpath. Bear-cub hoped his turn would come by the time he was fifteen. If he was fortunate enough then to count coup, the Lumpwoods, the Foxes, the Big Dogs, or the Muddy Hands would ask him to join their club—a man's club. That would mean that he was grown up.

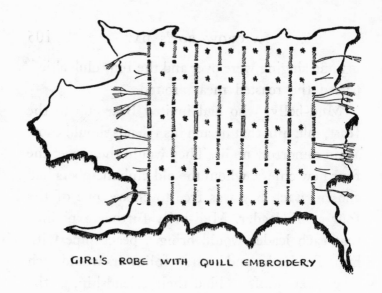

GIRL'S ROBE WITH QUILL EMBROIDERY

5

A CROW GIRL'S DAY

A Crow girl's childhood was short. When she was only seven or eight years old, she began to care for the younger children in the tipi and to help with the cooking and sewing. Mother, Grandmother, and Mother's sisters were glad to teach the little girl the skills they knew. By the time she reached the age of fourteen or fifteen, a Crow girl had had experience in all kinds of women's work. At fifteen or sixteen she was ready for marriage and able to care for her own household. Her childhood flowed smoothly. She was happy playing with other little girls and boys, helping her mother, and caring for her brothers and smaller sisters.

A Crow girl began her day with household chores and the care of the younger children. Inside the tipi lived her immediate family—her mother, father, brothers, and sisters. Often her father's second wife and their children also lived in the same tipi. Her father's second wife was usually her mother's sister. The girl liked her as much as she did her own mother and often called her Mother, too. The second wife had helped raise the girl and had cared for her when she was little. Similarly, a girl was glad to care for her second mother's children, whom she called Brother and Sister.

There was usually a grandmother or some other old woman or old man in the tipi. Old people preferred to live with their married children or other relatives rather than live alone. A Crow family had to take care of all its needs, and it was hard for a single person to live alone and provide every-

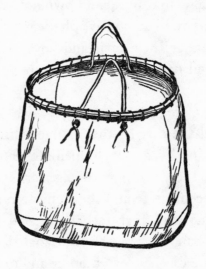

WATER   CONTAINER

thing he or she needed. Everyone, young and old, liked to have someone to talk to and to laugh with as they worked.

Meadow-lark was now about fourteen years old and already as tall as her mother. When she woke up in the morning, she slipped into her everyday buckskin dress and moccasins and ran to the river for a bath. If the neighbors' small children wanted to bathe, she took them along. The Crow liked the water, and there were always people swimming and playing or working by the river.

The women and children bathed and swam in a special place where the water was shallow. The men and boys had a place for themselves. The women also kept a clear place upstream where they got their drinking water. Way downstream, they often blocked off small sections of the river to soak buffalo skins and deerskins for tanning. Meadow-lark took along a small container made out of buffalo hide when she went for her morning swim and fetched fresh water from the river for drinking and washing.

Her mother, in the meantime, had put more chips on the fire and brushed off the stones she had been heating. These she put into a skin bag with water. As the water began to boil, she added the rabbit meat which Bear-cub had brought in the night before. She also put in some dried berries to make the stew more tasty.

Mother was her own happy self again, as she

had been before Eagle-claw's death. She hummed to herself as she worked by the fire and held her sister's baby in her lap. Mother's sister, her sister's husband, and their baby boy had moved in with them soon after the big buffalo hunt. So now the tipi was full of people and activity. The two sisters worked by the fire and talked and sang together. The baby was just beginning to toddle, and Meadow-lark was glad to have a baby to care for, as most of the other girls did.

A Crow baby, if healthy, did not cry much, and the Crow did not like to let their babies cry. When the baby cried, it meant that it was either hungry or wet, or both. Then Meadow-lark untied the soft buckskin straps that held the baby in its cradleboard and put fresh dry moss or grass, which served as the baby's diaper, under it. She placed the baby on its back in the cradleboard and tied it securely.

A cradleboard was really two layers of hide which had been sewed together. It was about a foot wide and about four feet long, and the head of the board was wider than the foot. In between the layers of hide, the women put twigs and curved them so they would hold the cradle's shape. The hood for the cradleboard was made of soft mountain sheepskin or buckskin and it was carefully embroidered with dyed porcupine quills. The women often added tassels of embroidered buckskin to the back of the hood.

A well-made cradleboard lasted long enough to serve several babies. Fresh buckskin was sewed onto the embroidered hood to replace worn-out skins. Unless the baby died, the mother kept the cradle even after she no longer bore children. Later she might present it as a gift to her daughter for her grandchildren. The daughter would be glad to have the cradle. To her, it meant that the babies raised on this cradleboard would be healthy, like herself and her brothers and sisters.

When Meadow-lark returned from her swim, the rabbit stew was simmering by the fire. Her mother's sister, whom Meadow-lark also called Mother, gave her some stew in a large spoon carved from a buffalo horn. Meadow-lark sat down near the baby and began to sip the hot liquid. She noticed that the baby was watching her as she picked a piece of meat out of her spoon and put it in her mouth. Perhaps the baby also wanted some meat—it tasted so good. The girl chewed the meat carefully. Then she put some of the

chewed meat on her finger and pressed the food to the baby's mouth. The baby sucked it off hungrily. Meadow-lark was much pleased. The little boy had not eaten meat before. She called to the women to watch her feeding the baby. Both nodded approval, so the girl quickly swallowed the piece she had intended for herself and began to chew another for the baby.

As soon as she finished eating, Meadow-lark picked up a small bundle of buckskins and unrolled it. This was to be a surprise for Bear-cub, and she worked on it secretly when he was away from the tipi. She was making a sheath for a knife. Their father had a steel knife, which he had traded from the Hidatsa for a horse. The Hidatsa told her father that the knife was obtained from the fur traders who were coming in from the north. At this time the Crow had very few metal objects and the knife was highly prized. Meadow-lark's father planned to present the knife to Bear-cub when he returned from seeing his vision. The boy and one of his friends were going to seek visions at the next full moon. Perhaps next summer, Meadow-lark thought, Bear-cub will be invited to join a war party. He will need a good knife then.

Meadow-lark had cut the buckskin and put a heavy piece of rawhide inside for backing. At first she did not hide her work, but now that anyone could see that it was a knife sheath, she worked only when her brother was away, so he would not suspect it was for him.

She took a handful of porcupine quills which her mother had dyed red and put them in a small horn cup filled with water, to soak. Then she took her small bone awl out of its embroidered sheath and began to make holes in the buckskin, resting the buckskin on a piece of hide. She put a few porcupine quills in her mouth and sucked them. Thus moistened, the porcupine quills became softer. Meadow-lark made two small holes in the buckskin with her awl, pulled the porcupine quill through the holes, and flattened the quill with her thumbnails.

She heard her friends calling and looked out of the tipi. "Come, bring your baby brother out," they said. "We have to watch the children. Their mothers are down by the river working on hides."

The younger children were in the midst of a game. They sat in a circle with their legs outstretched. One little girl stood in the center, her eyes shut tight. She turned in place four times and, as she turned, she tried to touch one of the outstretched legs with her toe. The children

moved away as the girl groped for their toes, but at last she succeeded in touching a boy's moccasin. Then she opened her eyes, the little boy climbed on her back, and she carried him outside the circle. The girl who carried away most children won the game.

Again she returned to the circle and shut her eyes. The children shifted to new places and yelled "Ready." Once more the little girl turned around four times, but this time she missed. The little boy returned to the circle, and another girl got up and stood in the center.

Meadow-lark continued embroidering the sheath as she watched the game.

One of her friends was sewing new soles of buffalo hide to an old pair of her father's moccasins. Another was sewing a second row of fringes to the sides of a new buckskin dress. This dress was going to be a marriage gift for a bride. The porcupine embroidery on the top of the dress was finished. As soon as the men drilled holes in some elk teeth, these would be sewn on the dress too. The three girls felt the soft white buckskin with their fingers and admired the beautiful dress.

Each one slipped it on and stood before her friends to be admired.

Some distance away several women were making a tipi cover. A cover was made of eight to a dozen buffalo skins sewed together with sinew. The most practical way to make one was for several women to work on it. So the bride's mother and her father's sisters worked together, while the bride and her friends cared for the children and cooked food for them. The skins were spread out on the ground, and the women sat on them and sewed. As usual, they turned the labor into a holiday with their laughter and gossip. They also teased the bride about her young man. "Did he ever strike coup?" "All I have ever seen in his mother's tipi was rabbit meat." "Did he ever get a deer, too, and maybe a buffalo?"

The young bride laughed with the women. It would never do to get angry or show that she was offended. These were her father's relatives and it was right that they should tease her and the bridegroom if they felt like it. Her mother's relatives would never tease her. That was against Crow custom. So she quietly answered that the young hunter had even led one of the raids against the Dakota. He had given her brothers several horses from that raid. He was very generous. Two of the buffalo skins in that tipi cover were his gifts to her mother. He had killed the buffalo in the last drive.

The girls listened to the jokes and laughter. "Elk-runner is going to speak to my brother about me next winter," one of the girls suddenly announced. "He spoke to me but I told him to wait. He says he'll bring my parents gifts as soon as he gets a few more horses. I don't want them to know, because my mother won't ever let me leave the tipi alone if she finds out about Elk-runner, and I do want to see him and talk with him. He wears the finest clothes and he's so handsome. He's not as tall as many of the men, but I don't like tall men."

"Nor do we," the girls agreed. "Tall men look like tipi poles," they said, laughing.

The young bride came over. "Never mind those women," the girls advised her. "They are gossips. Nothing to do but sew and talk, talk, talk."

"We'll be like them some day—fat and wrinkled," said Meadow-lark.

"If I could sew as well as some of those old wrinkled ones," her friend answered, "I wouldn't mind being wrinkled. I can't even punch a hole with my awl through those tough skins."

"Let's go play a game. I've made a new kickball," said the bride. "I'll get Younger Sister to watch the children for you." The girls rolled up their sewing carefully and took it inside a tipi.

There was a flat clear place behind the tipis, just right for their game. The ball was made of an antelope bladder filled with buffalo hair and covered with sinew. The bride picked it up and kicked it. She kept kicking it up with her soft moccasins and running after it till the ball dropped to the ground. Meadow-lark picked it up next and began to kick it, with her friends giving her advice. "Not so hard." "Not so high." "You'll miss that one." "Run, run." They were soon out of breath.

"Your mother calls you." A little girl came up from the river with this message for Meadow-lark. The game stopped. The bride returned to the group of women who were working on the tipis. One girl remained to watch the children, while Meadow-lark followed her friend down to the river.

A buffalo hide was stretched out on the bank with the hairy side underneath. The women had pegged stakes through it into the ground to hold the hide in place. Three women were working on it. Each scraped the flesh from the hide with a flesher, or scraper, made of elk antlers.

In a skin bag there was a mixture of buffalo brains, roots, and sagebrush. Meadow-lark began to rub this mixture into the hide. This softened the flesh and made it easier to remove it. The other girl went down to the river and brought up a bag of water. Then she washed off the scraped hide. Where scraps of flesh remained, she scraped them off with a small, sharp stone scraper.

The women had been scraping the hide since morning. It was late afternoon now and they were anxious to finish. When the girl finished washing the entire hide, the women began to pound it with a stone. This would finish the day's tanning.

Next day, when the hide dried, they would return and pound it some more. Then they would wash it with hot water and let it dry for another day or two. When the skin was dry, after the last washing and pounding, they would rub every bit of it between their hands to make it soft.

In the meantime, the hairy side of the skin had become more and more dirty, and it had not been very clean in the first place. To clean it, the women began by drying the damp hair before a fire. Then they shook the skin and beat it with sticks. The next step was to stretch a sinew rope between two poles and pull the hide back and forth over it, up and down, up and down. This helped clean the hair still more.

Next they sewed up the little holes in the hide made by the stakes and rubbed white sand into the scraped side of the skin. After this the skin was dried and pulled over the sinew rope again. At last the buffalo robe was finished.

Deerskins and the skins of mountain sheep had to undergo the same tanning treatment. These, too, took many days of labor. First the hair had to be singed over the fire and then both sides had to be scraped. The buckskin and mountain sheep-

skin were so much thinner that a woman had to scrape them very carefully.

Buffalo robes were not smoked, but buckskin and mountain sheepskins were. Tanning these skins called for an extra step. Meadow-lark had often helped her mother with the smoking. First they built a small rounded frame of twigs and branches. Then Meadow-lark made a little fire pit in the center and put rotted wood in it. They draped the buckskin tight over the frame, so no smoke would escape, and lit the fire inside. After the skin had been smoked on one side, they turned it over and smoked the other side. The smoked buckskin was then rubbed with a large pebble to make it smooth and give it a slight sheen.

The sun was setting and it was time to return home. Women and girls did not feel safe staying out after dark unless menfolk were with them. They left the buffalo skin to dry, took their scrapers and the skin bags, and hurried back to their tipis.

The men were returning home too. One had a deerskin full of meat tied to his saddle, another an antelope. Boys were returning on foot with rabbits, birds, and other small game they had caught. For a while the camp was noisy as children ran to meet their fathers, and dogs barked, greeting their masters. Then there was silence, as men, women, and children went into their tipis.

Inside the tipi where Meadow-lark and her family lived, the men and Bear-cub rested by the fire, while Meadow-lark and the two women were busy roasting fresh venison for the evening meal. The men talked and the women listened. Meadow-lark still had much to do. She helped serve the meal, cleared away the food, helped put the baby to sleep, and finally sat down by the fire to mend a pair of her father's moccasins.

Before going to sleep, while their mother sat working by the fire, Meadow-lark and Bear-cub asked her to tell them a story. The Crow knew many stories and legends. Some legends told how the earth came to be, how the animals were created, and how the Crow became a tribe. Other stories were intended to amuse the children. These were mostly about Old Man Coyote and his pranks. Meadow-lark listened carefully to these stories, so she too could one day tell them to her children. Her mother began.

"Long before there was any kind of land, there lived four little ducks. The Creator sent the little ducks one after the other to bring him some dirt from the bottom of the water. Then the Creator would take the dirt and see what he could do with it.

"When the fourth and bravest duck returned, it brought some dirt in its beak. This the Creator put into the palm of his hand and blew in every direction. Thus he made land, mountains, and rivers. Then he blew on his hand again and made a man and a woman. That is how the Crow were created. He then made deer, elk, buffalo, rabbits, foxes, and all the other animals, so the Crow would have meat and clothing. He also created fruits and berries.

"The Creator next killed a buffalo, cut it up, and explained to the Crow how to use all its parts. He showed the man how to make bows and arrows, axes, knives, and cooking vessels. He showed the woman how to cook buffalo meat, how to scrape a skin with the buffalo's foreleg, and how to sew the skins with sinew for clothing. He showed the man how to make fire with two sticks and some buffalo chips.

"At first the Creator did not make horses for the Crow. The people used dogs to carry their things. But the Creator told them how to get horses. He told them to go up a certain hill, but never look back. The men went up the mountain and wandered for four days. On the fourth day they heard horses coming up from behind. One of the men turned around, and the horses vanished.

"The men were very much upset, but the Creator said: 'Go up the mountain again. Cut pieces of flesh from yourselves and give them to me. Fast while you are on the mountaintop. Then I will come to you in your visions and tell you what to do and how to get horses and the things you need.' And that is how it has been ever since.

"The Creator also said: 'This land I gave you is the best land I have made. You will find everything you need on it: water, timber, game, and wild plants. I have put you in the center of this land and I shall put people all around you as your enemies. If I had made many more of you, you would be too powerful and you would kill the other people I am going to create. So I have made only a small number of you, but I have made you brave. So you may live long and enjoy the land I have made for you.' And so it has been ever since."

Bear-cub begged for a Coyote story. The mother continued.

"Old Man Coyote wanted to see how the Crow Indians were getting on. So he started for the Crow camp. On the way he saw a mountain goat and made it into a beautiful horse with red ears and a yellow rump. He ordered the horse to prance, paw the ground, and neigh as soon as they got into the Crow camp. Old Man Coyote then took a piece of bark and made a fancy saddle, bridle, and other fine trappings for the horse. He made a saddle blanket out of a leaf. It looked as handsome as a mountain-lion skin.

"Next Old Man Coyote dressed himself up. He mixed dirt and painted himself. He made himself leggings, moccasins, and a fine shirt with porcupine-quill embroidery. He covered his chest with shell necklaces. He braided his hair so it reached to his ankles. He made himself an eagle-tail fan out of grass and a coup stick of a buffalo rib.

"These preparations took Old Man Coyote some time. This was in the old days before the Crow had learned to make ornaments. Old Man Coyote invented all these things. By the time he reached the Crow camp, the sun was setting and everyone was returning to camp. Old Man Coyote was so heavily decorated that he could hardly move. His horse began to prance, paw the ground, and neigh as soon as they got inside the circle of tipis which made up the Crow camp. Everyone stopped to stare at the handsome rider. He looked neither to the right nor left, too proud to notice anyone. The children called to their mothers to come out of their tipis. The women rushed out and stood fascinated. Never before had they seen so handsome a rider.

"As the Crow began to move closer to the rider and his horse, the horse shied. Old Man Coyote was unable to keep his seat, because of all his heavy finery. He tumbled off the horse and fell into the dusty road. The women screamed. This frightened the horse even more. It turned into a mountain goat and ran away.

"The people quickly guessed that Old Man Coyote was up to his old tricks. They all rushed up to him to touch him, for everyone knows you can get some of Coyote's magic powers by touching him. But Old Man Coyote turned into a wolf and ran off. As he ran, he dropped his fine clothes. The people grabbed for them, but as soon as they touched them, the clothes turned into bark and grass.

"But to this day men still recall how handsome Old Man Coyote looked and how much the women admired him. That is why they try to dress up in all their finery when they want the womenfolk to look at them."

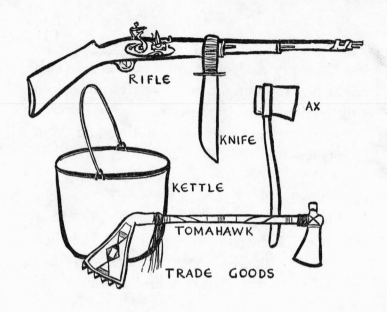

RIFLE

KNIFE

AX

KETTLE

TOMAHAWK

TRADE GOODS

6

THE CROW TODAY

TOWARD the close of the eighteenth century, English and French-Canadian trappers and fur traders began to come into the northern plains to trade for beaver and buffalo skins. At first the Crow did not come into direct contact with them. Instead, the Crow traded with their friends, the Hidatsa and the Mandan, and even with their enemies, the Cheyenne, when they were not fighting them. These tribes traded the European goods they got from the fur traders for horses and for the excellent skins and buffalo robes the Crow prepared. The Crow were getting horses by trading with and raiding the tribes to the southwest.

Trading took many days and was accompanied by many ceremonies and dances. Since the Crow had to travel a long distance to get to North Dakota, where the Hidatsa lived, the entire camp moved and camped near a Hidatsa camp. First the Crow set up their tipis and built their fires. Then the warriors, dressed in their best and riding their fastest mounts, charged into the Hidatsa camp. The Hidatsa lined up to watch and admire the Crow riders showing off their horsemanship.

The next day, the Hidatsa warriors, also dressed in their very best, charged into the Crow camp. The Crow, in turn, lined up to watch the Hidatsa riding. The Hidatsa horsemen were not as daring as the Crow and their horses were not as good. However, the Crow cheered them politely.

Trading began on the third day. The Crow who

were going to trade that day trooped into the Hidatsa camp, loaded with skins; buckskin shirts;
embroidered leggings, moccasins, and dresses; and
buffalo robes. Crow boys rode about, keeping
together the large herd of horses they wanted to
trade.

After the Crow laid down the articles they had
brought, the Hidatsa brought out large quantities
of trade goods: metal knives, axes, kettles, beads,
cotton goods, guns, and ammunition. On top of
their piles of goods the Hidatsa laid a beautifully
carved pipe, the pipe of friendship.

Before beginning to exchange their goods, a
Hidatsa chief lit the pipe and, after taking a few
puffs, passed it around to the Crow chiefs. While
the chiefs talked, both sides carefully compared
the articles they had brought with those that were
being offered to them in trade. When they were
satisfied that the exchange was fair, the Crow got
up and began to dance. Then the Hidatsa danced.
Each tribe watched the other with nods and smiles
of approval.

When the dancing ended, each chief picked
up the articles exchanged, and distributed them

among his people. Each family received its share, depending upon the amount of goods they had brought with them.

The Crow men and women quickly learned to use the metal knives they got and to cook their food over the fire in metal kettles. The women learned to use glass beads and needles in embroidery, instead of porcupine quills and awls. Young men could now go to the woods and quickly chop down trees for tipi poles with their new axes. They could shape bows and arrows with their sharp knives. They still preferred to use the bow and arrow when hunting buffalo, but they traded for guns and ammunition when they planned to go to war.

Early in the nineteenth century, the French-Canadian fur traders began to come directly into Crow country. By that time the Crow had grown to depend on European goods and they welcomed the traders. In 1807 a trader named Manuel Lisa built a trading post at the mouth of the Big Horn River—the first European building erected in Montana. For over fifty years the Crow enjoyed unusual prosperity.

In 1833 when the German explorer, Prince Maximilian, visited the Crow, their population had grown to about 4500. The men were trappers now as well as hunters. However, whenever they had a chance to strike out against their ancient enemies, they did. They still counted coup and each boy still wanted to become a warrior. The Crow warriors began to hold on to their goods and horses, instead of giving them away as they would have done in the old days. Many Crow chiefs were becoming very rich and no longer thought that generosity was important. They were becoming selfish.

The booming fur trade and the coming of the Europeans to the plains resulted in greatly increased slaughter of the wildlife: deer, elk, antelope, and, above all, buffalo. Buffalo robes and hides were in great demand. The settlers and the army needed the meat for their food. Farmers ground the bones for fertilizer. So the buffalo were killed off by the thousands. They were driven over cliffs and hunted with special high-powered guns called buffalo guns. Everyone killed more buffalo than were needed and let the extra carcasses rot. Out of an entire buffalo, hunters sometimes used only the tasty meat of the tongue and let the rest go to waste.

The buffalo herds began to disappear from the plains. The years 1880 and 1881 are those named as marking the disappearance of the buffalo. Actually, the buffalo did not disappear suddenly like a magician's rabbit, which is in his hat one minute and gone the next. Millions of buffalo were killed. Each year fewer and fewer calves were born. Slowly the plains were emptied of their buffalo herds.

As the European settlers moved westward, they pushed the Plains Indians toward the northwest, toward the mountains, into drier, poorer lands. Railroads began to be built, cutting up the open plains into sections. These sections were now the private property of the settlers and the Indians were told to keep off.

The Crow, who remained in southeastern Montana, began to feel the pinch of hunger as the buffalo herds thinned. Deer, elk, and antelope were now being hunted more and more and were also becoming scarce. Indians from the east were pouring into the western plains—all looking for food for their hungry people.

"Get the whites out of our lands," became the battle cry of most of the Plains Indians. "Let us unite for a war against the palefaces."

The Crow were one of the smallest tribes. For many centuries they had fought the Cheyenne and Sioux. The Crow now saw that these mighty tribes were losing to a mightier enemy, who had an endless supply of guns and ammunition. So the Crow chiefs offered their friendship and help to the American army. As a result, the Crow Indians are the one tribe of Plains Indians that has always been at peace with the United States. The Crow knew the plains well. Their warriors acted as scouts for the army and as guides for the wagon trains crossing Montana.

Montana, the Land of the Shining Mountains, the third largest state in the union, is still one of the richest. Gold, silver, lead, copper, zinc, petroleum, manganese, coal, and natural gas are found in it. There is farming and grazing land, too. Gold discovered in southwestern Montana in 1858 started a boom. Gold miners, pioneers, and

adventurers trekked westward, first to Gold
Creek, later to Grasshopper Creek, and then to
Alder Gulch. There the famed Virginia City,
now a ghost town, sprang up almost overnight.
At the same time gold was discovered at Last
Chance Gulch, where Helena, the capital of
Montana, now stands.

Other Plains Indian tribes, such as the Sioux,
the Cheyenne, and the Dakota, united against the
incoming settlers. They attacked, looted, and
wrecked trains and wagons heading for western
Montana. The American army pursued these Indians and fought skirmish after skirmish, battle
after battle, till the Plains Indians were defeated.
One of the last battles was fought on June 26,
1876, and is perhaps best remembered.

George Armstrong Custer, a graduate of West
Point, was a dashing young cavalryman who had
fought in the Civil War and eight years before
had defeated a large force of Cheyenne Indians.
When trouble began to brew in Montana Territory, Custer and his regiment were sent ahead to
investigate. The main army was to join him two
days later.

When Custer and his men came to the valley where the Little Horn meets the Big Horn River, they saw an Indian camp. It looked to Custer like a small Sioux Indian camp. He must have thought he had more than enough men to attack the camp quickly, destroy it, and win glory for himself. Even though his orders were to act as scout and wait for the army to catch up to him, Custer told his men to get ready for an attack. He divided his regiment into three columns. Two of the columns were to encircle the camp while Custer's column plunged into the valley directly toward it.

Custer was mistaken in his reckoning. A large force of Indians had hidden when they saw the army approaching, and were ready for the attack. As Custer reached the camp, he and his men were quickly surrounded. Custer was killed, and so were all the men in his column. Many of the men in the other two columns were also killed. Here and there, the Crow warriors fought off the Sioux and Dakota and rescued many of the wounded Americans from being trampled to death and scalped.

Soon the Crow willingly made a treaty with

the United States government and went to live on a reservation. Their reservation was very small compared to the lands they had once owned. About one hundred thousand square miles in what

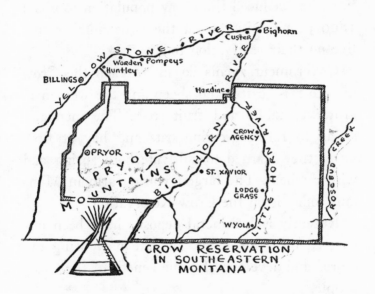

CROW RESERVATION
IN SOUTHEASTERN
MONTANA

is now southeastern Montana and northern Wyoming once belonged to them. It was a rich, varied land of streams and rivers, high snow-capped mountains, plateaus, and valleys. But seeing the fate of the other Indians, the Crow accepted the tract allotted them in southeastern Montana, a tract about eighty miles long and fifty miles wide. This region incorporates the Crow ancestral lands and their beloved Little Horn Valley and Big Horn Valley. Hunger, disease, and wars, by this time, had reduced the Crow population to about 1800 people—just about the same number that live on their reservation today.

Government agents began to teach the Crow men to raise cattle and sheep and the women to grow vegetables and fruit trees. The men also began to farm, growing oats and hay at first. Later they learned to cultivate both spring and winter wheat. The largest wheat farm in Montana today is on the Crow Reservation.

Recently rich mineral deposits have been uncovered on Crow lands, and are now being explored and developed for the benefit of the Crow people.

The government agents also helped the Crow build permanent houses instead of tipis, since the Crow no longer lead a nomadic life, following the buffalo herds. The Tribal Council wanted schools and hospitals. Crow delegates were sent to Washington to ask for more money for them.

The government teachers not only had to teach the children, but also the mothers. The Crow women had to learn about a better diet for

their children and themselves. The government doctors and nurses had the big job of teaching the Crow about health and modern medicine.

Today the Crow are very proud of their schools and hospitals. They are also proud of the wildlife on their reservation: buffalo, deer, elk, and bear. The buffalo herds are getting larger. The Crow

Tribal Council sees that no game is killed out of season. They hope that eventually the herd will supply enough meat, as of old.

In 1903 the Crow began to hold state fairs. These have become annual events. Everyone on the Crow Reservation comes to the fairs, as do the Cheyenne, Shoshone, Sioux, Blackfoot, and many other tribes from neighboring reservations. But the Crow plan the state fair, and only Indians can take part in it. There are parades and races and archery competitions. There is calf roping, bronco busting, and buffalo riding by Indian cowboys. In the evening there are Indian dances and singing. Men and women exhibit steers, sheep, and pigs, garden produce, and poultry, for which the Tribal Council offers prizes. Education Day is always marked by a parade of Crow school children, who exhibit the arts and crafts they have learned in the government schools.

Many men who still own beaded buckskins, leggings, and eagle feathers wear them to the fair. The women often wear buckskin dresses and shell necklaces. Most of them still wear moccasins. Pick-up trucks are very popular with the

Crow. Whole families come in them to camp at the fair. However, here and there, a family will come on horseback, wearing their best buckskins and beads and proudly carrying their garden produce on a travois.

The last day of the fair is give-away day. Everyone feasts on fresh buffalo meat which has been prepared for all of the visiting tribes in the true spirit of ancient Crow hospitality.

INDEX

INDEX